SMOKING OF FINE CIGARS

Fine, hand-made cigars, after they have been sorted by the color of the wrapper, are put into cedar cabinets and aged. The length of time they are aged contributes to the cost and quality of the cigar.

By Dr. Herbert R. Axelrod

A GUIDE TO THE SELECTION, CARE AND SMOKING OF FINE CIGARS

The author, Dr. Herbert R. Axelrod, on the right. The gentleman in the center is the manager of the Melia Cohiba Hotel in Cuba. The gentleman on the left is a famous cigar smoker. The photo was made in 1995 at the party celebrating the 150th anniversary of the Partagas brand.

© 1997, © 1998 TFH PUBLICATIONS, INC.
1 TFH Plaza
Neptune, N.J. 07753 USA

Completely manufactured in Neptune, N.J. USA

Second Edition

A GUIDE TO THE SELECTION, CARE AND SMOKING OF FINE CIGARS

QUALIFICATIONS OF THE AUTHOR

The author, Dr. Herbert R. Axelrod, has a Ph.D. (medical mathematics) from New York University (1961) and a D.Sc. (hon) from the University of Guelph in Guelph, Ontario, Canada where he is also an adjunct professor in zoology. He has written many texts in the fields of ichthyology (fishes) and classical music and has amassed an enviable collection of violins (all of which are on loan to eminent violinists or on display at the Smithsonian Institution.)

He has been involved in tobacco cloning and genetics in cooperation with Rutgers University and the Ministry of Agriculture in Cuba. He has sponsored an exchange of scientists between the USA and Cuba and has personal access to an experimental tobacco farm in Cuba where he cooperates with Cuban scientists in the production of genetically engineered cigar tobacco, especially the wrapper (capa). He is also involved with the Havana Aquarium in a similar role conducting research into the fishes in the marine and freshwaters of Cuba. He is still growing cigar tobacco in New Jersey where he maintains a genetically pure strain of wrapper black tobacco which, at the time of this writing, is producing its 45th inbred generation. This helps in producing tobacco plants which are predictable in size, color, leaf shape, leaf characteristics (such as the veins in the leaf) and taste. He is constantly comparing tobaccos, and the cigars from which they are made, from all parts of the world.

At 70 years of age and having smoked cigars for more than 50 years, he inherited this habit from his father and fraternal grandfather who owed their cigar smoking abilities to wives who allowed them to smoke freely in their homes. His wife allows him to smoke in their home. This is a VERY important consideration because smoking cigars should not be a nervous, addictive habit. It should be a period of relaxation and contemplation. That was the main purpose of smoking tobacco 500 years ago when Christopher Columbus discovered the Americas and the Amer-indians smoking tobacco. So seriously did the Amer-indians take their smoking ritual, that the term *peace pipe* was added to the English language.

SELECTING A CIGAR

The experimental cigars made under the author's supervision in Cuba. Their taste and aroma was judged according to the color of their wrapper. The aroma and taste of a cigar are determined by the wrapper.

SELECTING A CIGAR

Like most other things in life, the selection of a cigar depends solely upon an individual's taste, financial ability and the availability of the cigar he (or she) wants at the time the cigar is desired. Generally, people who smoke more than one cigar a day, prefer a progression of cigars in which the mildest cigar is the first smoke and a heavy cigar is the last smoke. **When** a person smokes a cigar is often conditioned by **where** a cigar can be smoked. Generally speaking, smoking of cigarettes is much more tolerated than smoking pipes or cigars. It is often difficult to find a place that tolerates cigar smoking. This is especially true of restaurants and other public places. It's up to you to find a relaxing spot where you can enjoy your cigar without causing any discomfort with the second-hand smoke produced by your cigar. That's one of the reasons that Havana cigars are so valued.

THEY SMELL GOOD.

My wife, who is a wonderfully tolerant person, has been exposed to many types of cigars and cigar smokers. She can tell a Cuban cigar just by the smell of smoke it produces. Her favorite expression is *My nose knows.* Keep in mind that the pleasant smell of a Cuban or any other cigar becomes foul and objectionable within a few hours, so some sort of exhaust must be available (usually an open window or door). A cigar butt also produces its own offensive odor if left overnight in an ashtray. I dispose of my ashes and butts in a toilet, first flushing it, then, as the water swirls around, I drop in the contents of the ashtray, butt and all.

Leaving the smoking to a later section, let's discuss how to properly select a cigar to suit YOUR taste and pocketbook. As I sit here writing in Cuba in May, 1997, I am amazed at the huge increase in the price of cigars during the past two years. Montecristo#2, the torpedo or pyramid shape, was offered for sale in the Partagas factory where they are produced in Havana, for $72.50 per box. All foreign transactions (tourist purchases) are done in U.S. dollars even though Cuba and the USA have had seriously degenerating relations since Fidel Castro's

SELECTING A CIGAR

socialist regime took over from the dictatorial regime of Batista. I priced them today and they are offered for sale at $120 per box of 25...and they are VERY hard to find. Worldwide demand for fine cigars seems to be doubling every year as cigarette smokers switch in the hope of being healthier because few people inhale cigars. Basically, smoking of any kind is injurious to your health, and if you are not a smoker now, don't start. Research indicates that cigar smoking may increse your risk of oral cancer.

B   JOYITAS   Nº.3   Nº.4   Nº.5

SELECTING A CIGAR

The fad of cigar smoking, will, hopefully, disappear shortly and will become an individual's pleasure rather than a sub-cultural fad. No more cigar magazines filled with cigar ratings which are misleading and uninformative; no more cigar dinners; no more beautiful ladies looking ridiculous on periodical covers smoking a big, fat cigar; no more proliferation of cigar books produced by prejudiced authors and publishers; no more astronomical rises in prices; no more fraudulent cigar labels.

Nº.1   Nº.2   ESPECIAL Nº.2   TUBOS   ESPECIAL

SELECTING A CIGAR

SHAPES AND SIZES

Traditionally cigars have been available in many shapes and sizes. I don't know any knowledgeable cigar enthusiast who smokes short, thin cigars, but many of the good cigar rollers in Havana smoke a single, rolled wrapper leaf in between their strong cigarettes. They usually smoke continually as they work. I don't know why there are so many shapes and sizes. I have preferences myself. For several important reasons the pyramid or torpedo shapes (Montecristo No. 2, for example) are my favorites. They seem to taste better. Thick cigars are always better than thin cigars because they usually draw better, smoke cooler and last longer. They are also more impressive (*the bigger the cigar, the longer the car* is an expession which indicates rich people smoke big cigars; big political and union bosses are typically shown in caricature holding a large cigar).

The shape of the Montecristo No.2 is called a *torpedo* or *pyramid* and is very difficult to roll. Only the most experienced rollers make this shape. These rollers at the Partagas factory in Havana roll 80 cigars per day.

It is very difficult to make a torpedo shape and very few rollers are able to do it. In the Partagas factory in Havana where 400 rollers (torcedors) toil, less than 10 can roll a good Montecristo No. 2. In Miami, Santo Domingo and New Jersey, the shortage of rollers who can make torpedo-shaped cigars is evident. Very few brands of cigar offer the pyramid or torpedo shape.

Most countries allow a tourist or resident to bring in 50 cigars duty free. It makes more sense to bring in large cigars than small cigars. I always bring in the longest, thickest cigars which I eventually cut in half before I smoke them. Many of my friends and I enjoy a short, thick

SELECTING A CIGAR

cigar called a *robusto*. This is a cigar about 5 inches long at maximum and a thickness of 48/64 to 52/64 of an inch in diameter. Like the jewelry industry, the cigar industry uses 1/64 inch between sizes. These sizes are called *ring* sizes. Thus a ring size of 50 is a thickness of 50/64 inch. Serious cigar smokers make friends

After rolling, the Montecristo No.2 are tied in bundles of 50 after having been color sorted. They are then aged for varying amounts of time depending upon demand.

Torpedoes, after being wrapped in binder leaf, are put into a mold for a short period of time before they are bound with wrapper (capa).

with local cigar rollers who usually can be depended upon to produce cigars to the size their customers prefer. Winston Churchill preferred long cigars about 8"long with a ring gauge of 50. Many makers call their cigars this size *Churchills*.

In order to make a cigar properly, a mold is required. Cigars can be made without a mold and every tobacco farmer in Pinar del Rio (Vuelto Abajo) in Cuba makes them without molds, but they usually vary in size and shape...but these farmer's cigars, usually made only from wrapper tobacco, are an extraordinary smoking experience. You can only evolve through experience to the size and shape you like best. Your best bet is the largest size you can get.

SELECTING A CIGAR

Cuban ex-patriots still roll hand-made cigars in Key West. They make special shapes which are paper-wrapped instead of molded because the molds don't exist for some shapes and sizes. It takes a very skillful roller to make cigars in this manner. Daniel had to pay $1 to get this photo. Photo by Jennifer Axelrod.

It may take a few hours to smoke. Just allow the cigar to go out and cut off the burnt end, saving the balance for the next smoke. Don't believe the story that you can't relight a cigar or save a cigar for another day. Try it yourself. It's just like re-lighting a pipe.

Once having selected the size and shape best suited to your taste, you have to go through the same process to find the tobacco which you like. Unfortunately, Cuban cigars are made in huge factories. There are six major factories in Cuba (Cohiba, Upmann, Partagas, El Laguito, Romeo y Julieta and La Corona) which produce roughly 100 million cigars a year (1996). These names have been changed to honor Cuban heroes. The H. Upmann factory has changed its name to Jose Marti and the bottom of each box made in this factory bear, the hand-stamp JM-XXXX. The X's indicate the month and year in which the cigar was made. It does not indicate the year it was harvested. To complicate matters, the original, pre-revolutionary owners still claim title to the brand names and you can find, for example, Montecristo cigars made in

SELECTING A CIGAR

Havana, the Dominican Republic and perhaps other countries of origin. The boxes look identical except for the tax stamp sealing the box. If in doubt, check the tax stamp. In general, tobaccos grown outside of Cuba can be depended

The Upmann factory in Havana, 1996.

upon to produce relatively uniform tobacco tastes. Thus, while there will be great variation in Montecristo cigars from Cuba as far as color and taste are concerned, they are still far superior to the Montecristos from other

The most famous Partagas factory in Havana, 1996.

The LaCorona factory in Havana, 1996. If you make a tour of Havana be sure to visit these factories and compare their wares.

SELECTING A CIGAR

countries even though the Cuban Montecristos are not hand rolled. In Cuba itself, the black market in cigars is huge and raging. You can be accosted on every corner if you walk down the street smoking a cigar. You can negotiate a box of Montecristo #2 for $30 while the price in the shop is $120! They are just as good as the real thing providing you check them carefully. Often the boxes are fake (so what!), but more often the top layer is 13 cigars but the bottom layer may be short 2-3 cigars! You are not advised to buy black market Cuban cigars anywhere in the world, especially Cuba. Tourists are restricted to buying cigars in official stores (tiendas) or from official demonstrators in hotel complexes or the airport. The quantity of cigars you can take out of Cuba is also restricted to $1,000 worth. However, customs officials at the Havana airport can be very generous in their interpretation of the cigar restrictions. You must show official receipts for all cigar purchases when you leave Cuba.

Most names of Havana cigars have been used to identify Dominican cigars. The only way to be sure of the country of origin is to examine a sealed box and view the tax stamp.

In other countries, cigar prices are negotiable except at the airports or in large stores. If you really love cigars, you'll be visiting all the cigar farms and factories every place your vacation or business trip takes you.

The Cuban cigar is the best in the world as far as taste and aroma are concerned. The quality of the Cuban manufacture suffers when compared to most other countries. They simply do not have enough experienced rollers in Cuba and, since they do not reward productivity with a higher wage, their individual production is low. The

SELECTING A CIGAR

average Cuban rolls 80 cigars a day; the average Dominican rolls 120 cigars a day; the average Cuban-American working in Miami rolls up to 150 cigars a day. The price of fine cigars worldwide has risen 200% from 1992 to July, 1997.

The taste of a cigar is hugely influenced by the condition of the cigar. Some smokers like dry cigars. Dutch cigars, for example, are as dry as possible and very hard. They are also small. The English taste is also predicated upon a dry cigar. Not as dry as the Dutch, but dry when compared to the original condition of the cigar in Havana. I like moist cigars. I want a cigar which burns slowly (=coolly), thus lasting longer. I make my cigars soft and moist by spraying them carefully with a fine mist and storing them in hermetically sealed, high quality plastic boxes. (I use Rubbermaid Servin' Saver..and I haven't been paid to say this!). I spray them very lightly once a day until they can be squeezed without cracking the wrapper. If you spray them too heavily you ruin the taste as the cigar *melts* and a dark brown juice flows from it. It takes skill and experience, so practice with cheap cigars until you have it right. There are moisteners which can be taped onto the top of a humidor or plastic box to give cigars a softer touch and more moisture.

A very productive Cuban roller can make up to 130 cigars a day, but they rarely do so because of shortages of wrapper or binder leaf.

THE CIGAR WRAPPER

Each cigar has a wrapper wound around it. Some cigars have the wrapper made of paper, a compound of paper and tobacco, or tobacco. The most difficult tobacco to grow is wrapper because every blemish in the tobacco leaf is exposed to view. Wrappers appear in

SELECTING A CIGAR

many different shades. Cuban experts say they separate cigars by the color of their wrapper...and there are at least 64 different categories.

Contrary to most writers, I have experienced a profound difference in taste between wrappers of different shades. Basically, the lighter the wrapper, the more mild the taste of the whole cigar. The only exception to this rule is the very, VERY dark tobacco they call *maduro*. Older books advise that this is a traditional Havana color. I have never found any maduro wrappers in Havana and the people who roll cigars tell me they don't know what happened to *maduro* wrappers as they have never seen any. Having smoked maduros, they are usually mild and full bodied.

Capa (wrapper) leaves are split in half by the removal of the central vein. During this process the leaves are separated by color.

Pre-revolutionary Havana cigars had the color of the wrapper stamped on the bottom of the box. That is no longer done, nor is it done anyplace else.

For my taste, I prefer a *colorado*, which is a dark brownish red. There are other terms used for wrapper shades such as: *colorado claro*, which is the usual color of non-imported American cigars. It is a brown color which can best be described by comparing it to other colors. *Claro* is lighter than *colorado claro*.

Double claro, previously called *fire-cured* is a green color which in the 1940's was THE color of the best cigars. It has a very light, mild taste. It is made by drying the leaves more quickly in barns which have small fires to generate heat and smoke. It can also be attained by cutting the leaves early and drying them quickly so they retain their chlorophyll (green) content.

It is practice to separate cigars by their colors in the cigar factories. Each box should be filled with 25 cigars

SELECTING A CIGAR

having the same color wrapper. The various leaves used for inside the cigar, fillers and binders, **which are not the basic** determiners of the taste and aroma, vary from one cigar to the other with barely more than random selection and availability of leaves.

Wrappers are the most important part of a cigar. They are often imported. The most important wrappers are grown in Connecticut, Cameroon (Africa) and Cuba's Pinar del Rio province. Cuba's wrappers originated a long time ago from Connecticut seeds. Tobacco grown from *Havana seeds* does not make a cigar taste like a Havana cigar. Havana cigars are so-called because they may be rolled in Havana but they are grown in other parts of Cuba. The world's best cigar tobacco, by far, is grown in the Vuelto Abajo region around Pinar del Rio. In 1995, the tobacco monopoly in Cuba started to change the name of Havana cigars to *Habanos*.

Previously you could trust what was written on the box as to the method of manufacture. Probably 35% of the world's cigar production is done with a small machine which rolls cut tobacco (tobacco chopped into pieces about an inch long) into a binder leaf. They are considered inferior but I am unable to tell whether a cigar is hand rolled or machine rolled just by smoking it. Obviously, machine made cigars are uniformly round. It is not possible to make a pyramid or torpedo-shaped cigar by machine. Maybe that's why this shape is so desirable?

Most of the cigars sold to the Cuban people for local consumption are

Finished cigars are sorted according to the color of the wrapper. This sorter is smoking a cigar as it is customary that people who make cigars can smoke them free of charge.

SELECTING A CIGAR

machine made and are cheap when compared to hand made.

HOW OLD SHOULD A CIGAR BE?

In most cases you don't know how old a cigar is when you smoke it. Some fine old houses (like Fuente) really do age their tobacco for three to five years before they use them for cigar manufacture. The Cuban Cohiba brand is supposed to do the same thing with three distinct fermentations. The coded date stamped on the bottom of the boxes of Havana cigars is real, but it doesn't say how old the tobacco is, just how old the cigar is. In discussing this with the president of the Cuban State Monopoly, he told me that they didn't age the tobacco for three years any more because the new type of Cuban tobacco developed by Eumelio Espino Marrero *"doesn't need aging and they have sold millions of them without a single complaint."* It's probably true. No complaints. A bad Cuban cigar is probably better than a good cigar from anyplace else.

For a wonderfully illustrated book on Cuban cigar tobacco you must read *CUBAN CIGAR TOBACCO, why Cuban cigars are the world's best* by Eumelio Espino Marrero, ISBN 0-7938-0294-6. It is the most honest and informative of any book about Cuban cigar tobacco.

But you never know for sure unless you order the cigar from the local cigar roller and mark it in some way to be certain it's what you ordered. The cigars I order are carefully made because of the parameters I set or requested. I use a colorado wrapper which is chestnut brown and I designate the kind of leaves I want for the filler and binder. To be sure that exactly those leaves are used, I request that the end of the cigar be left untrimmed...with a *moustache.* In this way I can be sure that the cigar is what I ordered. I only order pyramid shapes and all as close to 9 inches (without the moustache) with a ring size of 50-52. I cut off the end of the cigar with special cigar scissors and carefully inspect the leaves from which the filler and binder are made. The darker fillers are more oily, thus more tasty and stronger. 25% of the cigar's taste comes from the filler. Practically nothing comes from the binder. Lighter

SELECTING A CIGAR

fillers are more mild. The amount of mixture dictates the taste. Very few dealers offer cigars made in this way because they clearly show whether the filler is long (the most desired) and prime (uniform color).

New cigars, just made that day, are terrible. They have been moistened to make them easier to roll and are, therefore, too humid (the term *humid* is used by the rollers themselves). I have smoked Montecristo No. 2 on several occasions from years 1968, consecutively, through 1995. The older the cigar, the more character it has (by character I mean you can actually taste the tobacco). Cigars must be properly stored to properly age, yet I have never smoked an old cigar that was bad PROVIDING it was properly re-humidified.

The proper way to smell a cigar is to hold its cut end to your nose. Of course it becomes sterilized when you light it.

The test I make for a cigar BEFORE I smoke it is to smell it. This is NOT done by holding it under your nose and smelling the middle of the cigar. You simply stuff the cut end of the cigar actually into your nostril. In this way you get the real smell. The more it smells like tobacco and gives you a pleasant sensation, the better it will be. If it has no odor it will have no taste.

After the smell test, I cut off the end which goes into my mouth and suck on it to see how it draws and to taste the air which is drawn through the cigar. If it has no taste unlit, it won't have a taste when it is lit.

17

SELECTING A CIGAR

1. It's a matter of personal choice as to shape, size and quality.
2. Smoke milder early in the day; strongest cigar after dinner.
3. The thicker the cigar, the more pleasurable.
4. The cigar must draw easily or it might give you a headache from sucking too strenuously and usually it keeps going out.
5. The lighter the wrapper, the milder the taste.
6. The best tasting and most pleasing aroma comes from Havana cigars, though Dominican cigars are, as a rule, better made.
7. Expect your tastes to change from day to day, hour to hour, so keep different kinds of cigars handy to suit your changing moods.
8. Keep your cigars soft; dry cigars burn too quickly and are too hot.
9. Don't believe the ratings of cigars found in cigar magazines. Cuban cigars, and many others, are made by size. The names affixed to these cigars are based upon demand and availability of bands, labels and boxes. The publishers of most magazines know this since they have visited the factories in Havana. It is quite common for the factory to take a Montecristo label from a batch of cigars and substitute another label. Montecristo labels are the cheapest labels to make because they are a single color and not embossed. 50% of the Cuban cigars sold are Montecristos.
10. Don't smoke a cigar less than one week old or more than 3 months old unless its more than one year old.
11. About 75% of a cigar's pleasant taste and aroma come from the wrapper. 25% from the filler. 0% from the binder

STORING CIGARS

There are many reasons for storing cigars and, depending upon the reason, the storage techniques vary. Let's say you have a box of cigars which will be smoked within one month. Let's assume you live in the temperate zone in a home which has to be heated in the winter and probably cooled in the summer. Those circumstances are the most harsh for cigars, but the most usual. People living in tropical climates where the humidity is almost always over 70% with temperatures usually over 70°F. don't need humidors at all. They can just keep their cigars without additional humidification or protection from drying. Every cigar must be protected from odors (such as cooking), insect sprays, perfumes, dust and insects.

If you intend storing cigars for more than 90 days, they should be sterilized against tobacco beetles. These beetles occur in fine cigars (for some reason they never attack cheap cigars!) as eggs. You can't see them. The eggs hatch and the adults bore their way out of the cigar leaving a hole. This hole usually destroys the draw of smoke, but it is easily repaired. By soaking the end of the cigar, which is normally cut off and disposed of, in your mouth for less than one minute, the

Imagine your disgust when you open a box of 20 year old Sancho Panzo torpedoes and find they have been riddled with damage from tobacco beetles. Don't despair! The holes can be patched with the piece of tobacco you cut off the end of the cigar.

STORING CIGARS

tobacco in the end can be unwound and used to patch the hole(s) made by the escaping tobacco beetles. I have had old boxes of Havanas reduced to black dust. Once I brought back to Cuba a box of cigars which had been attacked by tobacco beetles and each cigar had two or more holes. The people at the Partagas factory were very kind and they wrapped the cigars with another wrapper...free of charge. This was, of course, during the pre-revolutionary times. The activity of the tobacco beetle increases with temperature. The eggs seem to hatch when the temperature in the cigar reaches 75°F. or more.

Tobacco beetles and other insects infesting tobacco leaves during their drying periods are normally killed by the gassing of the tobacco in a fumigation chamber for 24-72 hours. I tried this once in my home and I became ill for a week after. Don't try it! Instead I now freeze the cigars for 3-4 days minimum. This has ALWAYS killed the eggs since I haven't had this problem in more than 30 years. Why wholesalers and tobacconists don't use this method is difficult for me to understand.

Storage also depends on the quantity and quality of the cigar.

This is the way the author keeps his cigars. The moisture proof plastic box is the best humidor.

There was a time when you could have confidence in the product claims on the cigar box itself. By keeping cigar labels identical except for the country of origin (using type which is usually so small that you easily miss it), a casual look cannot tell you too much about the cigar. Fine Cuban cigars used to proudly proclaim HECHO A MANO. This meant (before 1989) that the cigar was 100% made by hand. Keeping the same cigar band and box labels, the stamp on the bottom of the box was changed to HECHO EN CUBA. This only means it was made in Cuba. It

STORING CIGARS

always means it was made by machine. We'll discuss methods of cigar manufacture in another section, but the whole point is that different cigars require different methods of storage.

The cheapest cigars are machine made with HTL. HTL stands for *homogenized tobacco leaf*. This is nothing more than bits and pieces of tobacco, finely ground, to which are added an aqueous mixture of gum Arabic or some similar gum. This is processed on a paper machine to produce tobacco paper. That's all that it is...a sheet of paper made from tobacco. I have seen entire cigars made of HTL. Just the thought of it is revolting. Obviously, cigars like this don't require storing because they are available every day at the local supermarket. Usually HTL is only used for binder and almost all cheap cigars are made using HTL binder.

Taking a sponge and putting it into a home-made plastic holder enables you to dampen the sponge and keep it in the humidor with your cigars to insure they don't dry out. The author has used this for 34 years!

The only cigars worth buying in advance are completely hand made cigars which you buy from a reliable source. Such a source may be a small tobacco shop in the Dominican Republic. The roller made a cigar especially for you and you loved it so you bought 500 of them never knowing if you would ever be able to buy any more. These are worth saving. They are actually easy to store. Simply freeze them for 3-4 days after placing them in a suitable air-tight plastic container. The container should hold 25 cigars. Write the date and identification of the cigar so you will remember how old it is.

Prior to opening the clear, plastic box and smoking a sample cigar, squeeze it to make sure it is still soft. If the sample cigar is hard and dry you have to re-humidify the whole box. This can be done in many ways. Having a lot of experience, I use a fine spray of distilled water. I spray all the cigars very lightly when I have taken them out of the plastic box and laid them on a white towel. I put each cigar

STORING CIGARS

back into the plastic box after massaging it gently to be sure there is no accumulated water which will *melt* the cigar and discolor the wrapper. Remember: most of the taste of a cigar comes from the wrapper. If you compromise the quality of the wrapper, you have compromised the taste of the cigar. How much you humidify a cigar is up to your personal choice. Many of my friends say I make my cigars too soft (=too wet). You can squeeze them as hard as you like and they will never crack. They complain that when the cigar is too moist it fails to stay lit. I don't have this problem as I smoke cigars rather quickly; but you'll soon learn how to use a mister.

There is a wonderful new invention on the market. It is a small plastic bag filled with water. The bag is glued to the top of the plastic container and slowly evaporates, keeping the cigars delightfully moist. You can achieve the same thing with cut pieces of apple. Just put the apple as far from the cigars within the plastic container as possible. The use of a piece of apple derives from using a piece of apple to maintain your pipe tobacco moist. Just shove the piece of apple into the depths of a one pound tin of tobacco. It works fine. However, though it works with cigars, it is a bit foolish when water works so much better.

This wonderful invention glues to the top of your humidor with two white adhesive strips on the plastic envelope. The water slowly evaporates from the envelope keeping your cigars moist. Contact Humatic Company, P.O. Box 250, San Carlos, California 94070 for the source nearest you.

A small espresso cup stuffed with a soft paper napkin and completely soaked with water can easily substitute for an apple.

I have never found any method of keeping fine cigars as humid as the day they were made in the Caribbean, Mexico or Honduras. When I bring them home to New Jersey I have tried a dozen methods and none work. I had wrapped

STORING CIGARS

each cigar in several layers of Saran wrap...to no avail. I have tied bundles of cigars in Saran wrap...to no avail. I have tried wrapping each cigar in Saran wrap and then storing them in an airtight plastic container. This is OK for a 3-6 month storage. I have used specially made cedar boxes in which I can store 100 cigars and I wrap that box in moist towels. All I do is create a nice fungus growth on each cigar. I just rub off the fungus and the cigar smokes perfectly. But if the wood gets too wet, the cigar melts and the wrapper degenerates, and you have ruined a fine cigar.

The optimum temperature and humidity is around 70% humidity and 72°F. I don't know of any portable humidor which maintains both temperature and humidity. They may have badly calibrated devices to measure temperature and humidity, but how do you adjust these physical factors? There is a way!

Farm stores and catalog houses offer special devices in which bird or turtle eggs are hatched. These are called *incubators* and they maintain temperature and

Granddad's leather-bound humidor, cedar lined, with a humidifier, circa 1912, was passed on from generation to generation. It NEVER kept a cigar moist enough to smoke! Sorry Dad.

moisture content. They even rock the cigars (=eggs) so the temperature and moisture are distributed evenly over the cigar. This device has only one weakness. It can't cool the cigar if the ambient temperature is too high! I solved that problem by keeping the incubator in an

STORING CIGARS

Aaron Sigmond, the editor of *Smoke* magazine gave me this 150 years old leather tobacco pouch. It is very hard and has a spring inside which keeps the cigars from moving. This can keep a cigar in smokable condition for 12 hours.

air conditioned room at 70°F. (My wonderful wife puts up with all of these little shenanigans!)

I'm sure there are many other ways that inventive people have found to keep their cigars properly stored. Tobacco dealers will store cigars for good customers, but I have ALWAYS found them to be too dry for my taste...but then how many people have a favorite tobacconist with the proper equipment who is willing to store *somebody else's cigars*. You would have had to buy your cigars from him (her) to have them stored. So if that is the case, simply buy a box of cigars every time you need it. If you want aged cigars, ask the tobacconist to hold and age them for you (and be prepared to spend a little more for this service).

While desk-top humidors are fine, expensive and decorative, they are absolutely not necessary for maintaining a cigar in a suitably humid condition. Lately, re-sealable plastic food bags became available at most supermarkets. Merely buy a box of suitably sized plastic bags. Put in your cigars with a damp paper towel; seal the plastic bag. Be sure that the wet paper doesn't touch any cigar and that there are no water drops to be absorbed by the cigars. If the cigars are dry and you want them to moisten quickly, put the bag where the temperature is highest. I use my

My son Todd, also a cigar smoker, gave me this sterling cigar holder. My initials are on the top of the cap. This can keep a cigar in smokable condition for 24 hours.

STORING CIGARS

furnace room, or lay them in the sun (inside the house). The cigars should be soft and ripe for smoking within a week or less.

STORING YOUR CIGARS

1. Don't waste your time with mass market cigars you can buy at your local supermarket. Just buy small quantities every few days and they'll stay the way they were when you bought them.
2. Fine cigars dry out quickly. A fine, moist cigar left on your desk for 5 hours can be too dry to smoke. Never leave cigars out in the air. Store them in air-tight plastic boxes or bags, even if you only store one or two cigars.
3. To carry a few cigars in your pocket, use a metal or leather pouch made expressly for this purpose. But in 24 hours the cigar will have deteriorated.
4. Freeze your fine cigars for 3 or 4 days to kill tobacco boring beetle eggs. Allow them to thaw completely before smoking them.
5. Air-tight plastic boxes or bags can be used for long time storage.
6. Cigars which have dried out can be re-humidified by misting or storing close to a water source. Only use distilled water as the fluorine and/or chlorine can alter the taste of a fine cigar.
7. Cigars with beetle holes can be patched.
8. Ideally, store your cigars at your tobacconist where he has a humidor which controls both temperature and humidity.
9. There is no known humidor for your home or office which CONTROLS both temperature and humidity (most humidors just MEASURE these parameters).

HISTORY OF THE CIGAR

In a simple sentence: *No one knows for sure how the cigar was invented.* The earliest documented mention of cigars was Columbus' description of *a roll of leaves in a leaf of itself.* The IRS uses this same definition which is, I suppose, very complimentary to Columbus. Columbus was credited with bringing some of these rolls of leaves back as souvenirs of the Indian life. Some of the young sailors on the boat obviously tried this weed out in the Caribbean where Columbus first landed, and the novelty spread. The history of cigars is the history of Cuba.

No one really knows how the name *tobacco* originated, though there are lots of theories. Some writers say the word originated with the Indians in Santo Domingo who inhaled tobacco smoke in a Y-shaped pipe stuck into their nostrils. This was called *tobago* (another Caribbean name) which was later written as *tobacco* by the English.

The word NIVELACUSO is the Cuban date code. The letters run from 0 to 9. Thus a stamp on the bottom of a box might read NIUS and that would translate into 12/89 or December,1989. This box was in the Davidoff warehouse.

I have spent a lot of time in the jungles of Brazil. Many of the Indians there use tobacco (and marijuana, hallucinogenic mushrooms, and other such goodies, cocaine included). They rolled the tobacco leaves onto themselves continuously until they had produced a rod that was about 6 feet long and 2-3 inches in diameter. They allowed this to age and harden and then shaved the end to produce cut tobacco which they smoked in crude pipes or wrapped in green tobacco leaves. I tried a few puffs and immediately became dizzy. Later on it dawned on me that this might not

HISTORY OF THE CIGAR

have been pure tobacco but might have had some hallucinogenic added.

In any case, no one knows for certain how the word *cigar* originated, though the Mayas of Mexico were credited with the word. I made two telephone calls to Mayan academic authorities and they disclaimed any such knowledge.

The Spanish occupied Cuba and began producing cigars for export to Europe. The French ambassador to Spain got hold of some Cuban tobacco seeds and France began producing tobacco. The name of the ambassador, by the way, was Jean Nicot, thus the word *nicotine*. By 1580 tobacco was being grown all over the world as it became a favorite drug, medicine and pastime for sailors. The growth of tobacco was better in France, Holland, Massachusetts, Virginia and the Carolinas than in the tropical world, but the taste was not the same. To this day one of the best cigar wrappers is grown in Connecticut, while exceptional cigarette tobacco is grown in Virginia and the Carolinas. Tobacco cultivation is a world-wide business and hobby. You can easily raise tobacco plants in your own home.

On November 2, 1492 Columbus discovered America and tobacco leaves. There are many renditions of this historical event.

The history of cigar making is extremely interesting and complex. The many steps it takes from seed to cigar were developed to such sophisticated levels it is a monument to the dedication of farmers, manufacturers and marketers. The love men (and women) have for cigars borders on fanaticism. For some, cigar smoking is one of life's greatest pleasures. My day is not complete without a strong after-dinner cigar. My wonderful wife leaves me alone during this

HISTORY OF THE CIGAR

time (my WA time...*wa* has a Japanese meaning of *contemplation*). I think about many things and the tobacco seems to enable me to focus my thoughts; cigar smoking is actually a sensual experience both in the smoking itself and the smelling of fresh cigar smoke. It all ends very abruptly when the cigar is dead for 30 minutes...then it becomes outrageously malodorous, as does the cigar smoke which is best evacuated with an exhaust fan. I know so many friends with small 6" exhaust fans cut into their windows.

For the more inquisitive reader there are three wonderful books about cigars. These books were written by Cubans. They are exceptionally well illustrated. The writers are authorities and the books have passed critical review. You can purchase (or order or review) these books at fine cigar dealers, libraries and large bookstores. Most cigar books are written by dealers of cigars. They know their cigar business very well but they only *push* their own cigars. Books written by Americans usually damn Cuban cigars and proclaim Dominican cigars as now being the world's best. It suits their purposes because they sell Dominican cigars and have no Cuban cigars to sell.

Cuba produced most of the world's supply of cigars at the turn of the 20th Century (around 1902 to be exact). They supplied the world with 350,000,000 hand rolled cigars. In 1997 they expect to sell 50,000,000. Americans bought 200,000,000 cigars in 1996 with 1,000 different brands and shapes from which to choose. The size of the cigar industry (which is tiny when

Cuban indians rolled tobacco leaves and smoked them in a manner similar to today's smoker.

HISTORY OF THE CIGAR

compared to the cigarette industry) is staggering. In 1868, right after the Civil War, Connecticut had 250 cigar factories and later on New Jersey had even more. Trenton, New Jersey was the cigar-making capitol of the world until Tampa, Florida took over and Ybor City became a reality in 1869 taking the business away from Connecticut because the Cuban cigar rollers preferred working and living in Florida than in Connecticut.

CIGAR HISTORY

1. No one knows who or how the cigar was invented. American Indians in South America and the Caribbean islands used tobacco.
2. Christopher Columbus brought the cigar to Europe.
3. *The name* NICOTINE derived from a French ambassador to Spain, Jean Nicot.
4. By 1580 tobacco was being used and grown worldwide.
5. Cuba has dominated the cigar scene for more than 400 years.
6. Cigar manufacturing came to Florida and New Jersey when the U.S. placed a restrictive import tax on finished cigars but allowed tobacco leaf in without restrictive duties.
7. One hundred years ago Cuba exported over 300 million cigars. In 1996 it exported 50 million.
8. Millions of cigars are smuggled into the U.S.A. because U.S. laws prohibit Americans from buying anything Cuban.
9. Best book on cigar history is HAVANA CIGARS 1817-1960 by Enzo A. Infante. ISBN 0-7938-0291-1. Available at any book or cigar store. It was published in 1997.

HOW TOBACCO IS GROWN

Cigar tobacco is basically grown the same way worldwide. Most of the cigar tobacco is grown in open fields; but the leaves for the wrapper are grown in the shade. Huge tents of cheesecloth or gauze protect the delicate leaves from excess heat, drops of rain, insects and anything else which may damage the leaf. In Cuba today (June, 1997) there are precious few leaves grown under cheesecloth. Most of it has been stolen for curtains and other purposes. There is a tremendous shortage of wrapper (capa) in Cuba as well as the rest of the world.

Vuelto Abajo, Cuba, tobacco is so valuable that every little patch of land is used to grow at least one crop of tobacco between September and March.

THE PARTS OF THE CIGAR

A fine cigar is composed of three general parts: wrapper, binder and filler. The wrapper and binder are generally half a single leaf. Almost all of the beauty, color, taste and aroma of a cigar comes from the wrapper. Cuba is the only country I know of which uses Cuban-grown wrapper, though they freely admit it was derived from Connecticut seed. Africa's western country Cameroon produces excellent wrapper, as does Honduras, Sumatra and (rarely) the Philippines.

The leaves for a cigar usually come from a different part of the same plant...but not always. In Cuba, where they are still making cigars the way they were made 400 years ago, there are daily examinations of most plants when the leaves are large enough to begin harvesting. Naturally, the largest leaves are taken off the plant, usually in pairs. The top leaves, often referred to as

HOW TOBACCO IS GROWN

ligero, or *corona,* are the heart and soul of a cigar. These are the darkest leaves, the most tasty and the most oily. I have had a small cigar rolled from a single corona leaf and it was delicious. The single leaf, though, smoked very fast and almost burnt like a cigarette, not extinguishing itself when it wasn't being drawn. The corona is an important part of the mix in cigar making because of the flavor it adds. It also keeps the cigar lit because it burns well. For this reason it must be placed into the center of the cigar. Poorly rolled cigars in which the corona (ligero) leaf is on the outside of the bunch, touching the binder, burn unevenly. Great cigars, the kind which used to be made in Havana in the 1950's, were produced using corona leaves 4-5 years old. They require this aging process because of their oil content. Good Havanas (or other greats) actually exude tobacco oil as a gas from their leaves as they mature. If you are lucky enough to have good cigars in their original cellophane wrapper you will notice that the cellophane becomes tan after a few years of holding a fine cigar.

A corona leaf, matured for 5 years and made into a cigar which is also matured for 5 years, produces a heavenly smoke.

A typical Cuban tobacco farm features sun-grown cigar tobacco, a shade grown tobacco for wrapper and a barn for drying the leaves. This layout could be typical of any cigar-tobacco growing country. They still do it the same way.

HOW TOBACCO IS GROWN

Of course cigars are made from other leaves from the same tobacco plant and occasionally corona leaves are utilized for binder as well as filler.

The center leaves are often referred to as *centro* or *seco*. There is tremendous variation in these leaves and some 17 are now recognized by the Cuban cigar trade and used for blending purposes. These are sophisticated in taste, neither strong nor mild. I have smoked cigars made from various secos and they have a pleasant taste. I like this taste for my midday cigar. It is used for blending to give certain cigars a characteristic taste.

Cuba has isolated laboratories in which special kinds of tobacco are developed. Eumelio Espino Marrero has developed several strains of tobacco which are resistant to most of the plagues which destroy tobacco crops.

In the olden days when individual entrepreneurs owned their own tobacco brands, a Partagas Churchill always tasted the same, from box to box. Now Cuban and other fine cigars are basically graded according to the color of their wrapper because 75% of the taste and aroma of a fine cigar derives from the wrapper. Specially fine seco leaves are used as wrappers. To be a wrapper (*capa* in Cuba), the leaf must be large, unblemished, small veined and uniform in color. Thus, if you choose a cigar by the color, texture and sheen of its wrapper, the cigar will taste the same as any other cigar whose wrapper is identical, REGARDLESS OF THE MANUFACTURER. To properly age, a seco leaf requires two years.

HOW TOBACCO IS GROWN

The bottom leaves on the plant are variously called the *volado* or *libra de pie*. They are essentially indistinguishable from the seco, middle leaves, except they are lighter in color and elastic. Being lighter in color means they contain less oil and it is the oil which gives cigars their characteristic taste. These elastic leaves are mostly used for binder. They burn easily so they are valued for helping a cigar stay lit in between puffs. The test of a good mix of wrapper and binder is the black ring at the base of the ash. The black ring should be as small as possible and be perfectly round with the binder, filler and wrapper burning in unison. There is nothing more annoying than a cigar which burns quickly on one side leaving the other side unlit.

Wonderful, healthy wrapper tobacco growing under the gauze tent which provides shade for the plant.

For the hearty after-dinner cigar, I prefer a dark reddish brown cigar which is strong. You can always depend upon a dark reddish brown wrapper to produce a strong, tasty cigar. This is one of the reasons (beside the visual effect) that cigars are sorted by the color of their wrapper. All cigars in a box should have the same color wrapper.

THE ROLE OF THE TOBACCO FARMER
Tobacco is a weed and grows like one. I have been keeping tobacco as a house plant for many years. I wait

HOW TOBACCO IS GROWN

Cuba's top tobacco expert, Eumelio Espino Marrero, at the entrance to an experimental gauze tent in which shade grown tobacco will be cultivated.

until it flowers and I cross-pollinate it with a mink paint brush. The ripened flower bears a seed pod in its base when the flower dries. This seed pod contains thousands of seeds each about the size of a ground pepper grain. It is common for a single tobacco plant to yield a few thousand seeds. The seeds can be planted as soon as their pod is dried, which is about one week. I have been in-breeding tobacco plants grown in the lobby of my office. I have the 45th in-bred generation of seeds. I also have the same generation of clones which I produce by clipping off a piece of the young plant and growing it in a special nutrient solution. This is a rather simplified version of cloning, but cloning tobacco is not difficult at all. Every one of my plants now grows over 8 feet tall and has soft, large leaves

HOW TOBACCO IS GROWN

almost all of which are of capa (wrapper) quality. Of course my office lobby gets very limited light, perhaps 1-2 hours of direct sunlight per day. Yet the tobacco plant thrives, even though the winter temperature may drop to 40°F. overnight. Tobacco is a hardy weed!

To grow the tobacco I take a seed pod and crush it between my fingers. I spread the seeds on the top of six 14" flowerpots filled with potting soil which I have carefully sifted to make it soft. Once I have spread the seeds I sift more potting soil on top of the seeds so they are covered from sight with perhaps $1/4$ of dirt. Then I spray the top of the flowerpot with tap water to which I add ordinary fertilizer (the kind suggested for tomatoes). I fertilize once a week until the plants are about half inch high. This takes about 10-14 days depending upon the temperature. The top of the flowerpot becomes completely covered with small plants. I then start spraying the plants themselves with the same weak solution of fertilizer. They absorb it through their leaves. I allow this beautiful carpet of green to grow

Tobacco diseases have plagued tobacco farmers for years.

A tobacco leaf ruined by disease. Many farmers still use these damaged leaves for the filler of the cigar.

HOW TOBACCO IS GROWN

for a few weeks and then I begin the weeding process. I allow the four largest plants to share each pot and throw out the seedlings (or give them to friends who are intrigued with tobacco). As they grow over one foot tall, their leaves become too heavy for their stem and they must be supported. I use thin tomato stakes until the plants are about 30" high, then I use a thin, cotton twine fastened to the ceiling. This has to be adjusted every few days as the plant is not a vine and must be twisted around the string as it grows. Grown in this manner, it becomes the ultimate in shade grown

The author, Dr. Herbert R. Axelrod, with the tobacco plants growing in the foyer of his office. Tobacco can be raised under most conditions suitable to other houseplants.

The tobacco leaves are sewn to each other at their bases and then hung to dry in huge sheds.

tobacco! It takes 3-4 months to flower.

I have observed tobacco farmers over a world-wide range. They all have their own techniques; the Cubans are the most primitive while the Connecticut farmers are the most advanced. They all go through the same steps described above, except they do it on a much more grand scale.

Seeds are sown onto a specially prepared bed. The bed is covered with hay (straw) to protect the seeds against birds and other seed-eaters and to break the water spray so it

HOW TOBACCO IS GROWN

doesn't disturb the seedlings. The roots of the first seedlings are very shallow and they are easily washed out. Cuban scientists use small plastic pots which are molded from a single piece of plastic. (The usual cups are those which are used for the single-serving cream for your coffee found in most restaurants.) Typically, the seedlings are protected in their beds until they are about six weeks old. The hay is carefully removed and the seedlings are transplanted to their fields of destiny. The planting is done according to a scheme because workers have to walk down rows between the plants to harvest, prune and fertilize. The leaves also must not touch each other as they can easily cause damage by the constant rubbing caused by the winds. Tobacco grows about 2" per day (hence I call them *weeds*). That means that in 7 weeks

Tobacco plants in Pinar Del Rio, Cuba, being transplanted from their germinating beds to straight rows with about 3 feet in between rows.

they are fully grown and flowering. To get greater leaf size the farmers clip off the buds before they flower. Harvesting is started when the plants are 4-5 weeks old. The largest leaves are usually found in the middle of the plant and the best of these are used as wrappers. In more modern farms the leaves are cut off the plants every day

HOW TOBACCO IS GROWN

A typical drying barn in Cuba. During the summer temperatures inside must be closely regulated. The doors and windows can be opened to reduce the heat and humidity.

depending upon their size. Various methods are used to take the cut leaves from the field. The Cubans do it by hand. They carry the leaves they cut, sometimes putting them into baskets. In Connecticut and some farms in Africa (Zimbabwe and Cameroon), they drop the cut leaves onto a long canvas laying on the ground. This is then dragged to the beginning of the row either by hand, by machine or using a bicycle-like device which brings in the liner. For our purposes, it doesn't matter how they do it. It is simply a matter of bringing in leaves of the same size. These gatherers walk through the fields, row after row, day after day, selecting the best leaves. If they are lucky, it won't rain too much, nor will it be too windy. In Cuba the growing time is from September to March. One crop is usual; very rarely two crops can be produced.

The large tobacco leaves are brought from the field to the curing barn. Curing barns worldwide vary, but essentially they are tall, windowless, scrawny buildings which are used to keep the light and insects out and the heat in. Inside the curing barns are women (usually) who take leaves of the same size and sew them together through

A typical tobacco farmer in Cuba. Tobacco farms normally lead rustic existences...remember the book *Tobacco Road*?

HOW TOBACCO IS GROWN

the heavy vein at the base of the leaf. These *hands* contain from 25-40 leaves (in Cuba; they vary in other counties). After the *hand* is formed, it is draped over a long pole which, when filled, is raised to the highest available space in the barn. It takes

The lack of spare parts has brought tobacco production to its lowest levels in Cuba's history. This is a view of a major farm in Cuba.

6-10 weeks for the first curing during which time the leaf loses its chlorophyll (green) coloring and changes to a xanthophyll (brown) coloring. It shrivels and looks like any dried leaf. The drying process is delicate. The leaves and the sealed barn give off heat which must be controlled by opening doors and creating drafts. This venting process is done by the master tobacco grower and is a 24 hours a day job. Less than 8 weeks later (usually 6 weeks), the leaves are removed from the poles and separated by size and color into bales. The bales vary in size by country and farm. The bales are left in a dark, sealed room to ferment. Again the temperature is regulated and each bale has an immersion thermometer which measures the temperature inside the bale. A temperature of about 110°F. is maintained.

One of Cuba's best producing tobacco farms uses these buildings for drying. Luxury it ain't!

Fermentation times vary from one to six weeks. After the first fermentation, the leaves are again sorted by size, color and quality. Leaves destined to be *capa* (wrapper) may not be stained with yellow water

marks, have any kinds of holes or be torn. The best wrapper leaves are re-baled, wrapped in huge bales of 1,000 pounds (my guess!), and allowed to ferment again. This time the fermentation process must last for a few years. The best leaves are stored in these bales for up to 5 years. The fermenting barns in Cuba are concrete buildings in the best of condition. They are guarded against theft as *capa* is the usual limiting factor in cigar production.

> **HOW TOBACCO IS GROWN**
>
> 1. Cigar tobacco leaves are grown worldwide except for the frigid zones. It is grown and processed in essentially the same way the Cubans developed the process 400 years ago.
>
> 2. There are three types of tobacco leaves. The top leaves of the plant are called the CORONA or LIGERO. The leaves growing from the middle of the plant are called CENTRO or SECO. The bottom leaves are called VOLADO or LIBRA DE PIE.
>
> 3. World's best and newest book on growing tobacco is *CUBAN CIGAR TOBACCO* by Eumelio Espino Marrero. ISBN 0-7938-0294-6.
>
> 4. The same seeds grown in different areas taste, smell and look differently.
>
> 5. No cigar leaf compares with leaves grown in Cuba regardless of their origin. Cigars which proclaim they are "Grown from Cuban seed" are usually misleading. Cuba (since 1971) has not exported seed. Even if Cuban seeds are smuggled out of Cuba, it's where they grow that counts.
>
> 6. You can easily grow your own tobacco as a house plant.
>
> 7. Tobacco is either field grown (lowest quality) or shade grown (highest quality).
>
> 8. Fine cigars are made from tobacco which is aged.

HOW A CIGAR IS MADE

Once the tobacco leaves have been aged, fermented, sorted, selected, baled and evaluated, they are once again fumigated and then shipped to factories. Interestingly enough, no cigar tobacco is grown in Havana City, though there are some tobacco farms in the areas close to Havana. Yet the world's best and most famous cigars are called *Havanas*, though 1996 saw a change to the name *Habanos* on the familiar boxes of Havana cigars. The reason for the term *Havanas* (pertaining to cigars), derives from the fact that most famous factories do their rolling of the leaves into cigars in the city of Havana. These factories were located in Havana because the owners of the factories chose to live in Havana, there was a greater concentration of population in Havana (greater labor pool), and because Havana was and still is the major port for the export and import of goods to and from the outside world. For a really interesting book about the famous cigar factories of Cuba before the Revolution, read *Havana* Cigars 1817-1960 by Enzo A. Infante, ISBN 0-7938-0291-1.

Cuba has cigar factories in Pinar del Rio close to where the tobacco is grown. They make the poorest quality cigars I have ever found in Cuba. They use the worst leaf. All of their output is sold to visiting tourists who want *Vuelto Abajo* tobacco or to locals who pay in local currency. The tourists get their Vuelto Abajo tobacco, but it is the tobacco rejected for export-quality cigars.

Cigar rollers have been temperamental artists and malcontents for centuries. Georg Bizet in his famous opera *Carmen*, portrayed the heroine Carmen as a cigar roller in a cigar factory in Spain! Yes, they had cigar factories all over the world, too. Very little tobacco was grown and rolled in the same area. Only Cuba uses its own leaves for the cigar, most other factories use wrapper from thousands of miles away, to say nothing of the binder and filler.

Since the rollers are such individualists, you'd expect their products to bear their stamp of individuality. They

HOW A CIGAR IS MADE

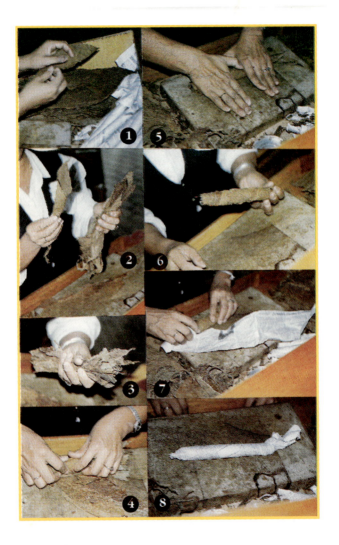

HOW A CIGAR IS MADE

do! I have favorite rollers who make the cigar the way I like them. They leave the ends of the cigar projecting so I can be sure the cigar is properly made. I don't want the cigar to be heavy on the draw; I don't want fast burning tobacco touching the binder or wrapper; and I want a cigar as laden with oily leaf as possible.

They taught me long ago that I must shove the cigar into my nostril to properly smell it; that I should taste it before I light it, etc. You have so much to learn from a roller. I call them *tobaceros*, but that is not a correct name. The roller is more properly called a *torcedor*. They produce from 75 to 150 cigars a day depending upon many factors, of course. Pyramid shaped cigars are much more difficult to roll than a panatela.

In any case, the best *ALL HAND MADE* cigars are made the same way. A number of leaves are selected and laid in the torcedor's hand the way you might accumulate a fist full of long feathers. The selected leaves have had their center vein removed because these veins take too long to burn. The *bunch* as it is called, is built so the leaves all lay in a parallel condition so the smoke travels up the length of cigar without obstruction. The top and bottom is torn off by hand so the bunch is, more or less, composed of leaves of the same length. These leaves are called *filler* leaves and are the least valuable of leaves taken from all parts of the tobacco plant. Wrapper which is torn or otherwise unusable can also be part of the filler. The selection of the leaves is pre-determined by the roller (*torcedor*) according to either a fixed formula or, more usually, from whatever leaves are available. Prior to making the bunch he (she) has laid a binder leaf on the table, stretched out and very moist so it is elastic. The bunch is then laid onto the binder leaf at about a 45° angle to the center of the binder leaf. The binder is then tightly rolled around the bunch, using about 3-4 revolutions to completely bind the loose filler leaves.

Left: HOW A FINE CIGAR IS ROLLED. 1. The large vein is removed from the leaf. 2. The leaves are rolled into long tubes and 3. gathered into a bunch. 4. The bunch is then rolled with a binder leaf to hold it together. 5. and 6. The bound bunch is then rolled to the general shape of a cigar. 7. The cigar, minus the wrapper, is then *'molded'* by rolling it with *newspaper* 8. where it is kept for a few hours until the capa (wrapper) is put on.

HOW A CIGAR IS MADE

This rough looking cigar is then put into a wooden mold for a few minutes to a few days (the last cigars on the weekend or evening are left for the next working day). This insures they are uniform in thickness and length. Then the wrapper is put on in a similar fashion as the binder. Depending upon the shape, the end of the cigar which goes into your mouth is either left on with the end twisted (farmers and very fancy brands use this technique) or small pieces of tobacco about an inch

---

HOW A CIGAR IS MADE

1. Cigars are usually not made close to where the tobacco is grown. The world's best tobacco comes from the Pinar del Rio province of Cuba but the best tobacco from Pinar is rolled into cigars in Havana, 100 miles away.

2. A good Cuban roller produces about 80 cigars a day. A good Dominican roller does 125-150 per day.

3. Rolling torpedo or pyramid shapes are the most difficult.

4. Wrapper tobacco is the limiting factor in producing more fine cigars.

5. Cigar boxes mislead with their labelling. Only modern Cuban boxes which are branded **TOTALAMENTE A MANO** are completely, totally made by hand.

6. HTL, homogenized tobacco leaf, is paper made from tobacco leaves and vegetable gum. It is used for mass market cigars as wrapper, binder and/or filler. There's nothing wrong with mass market cigars if you like them. They usually sell for $2 or less while a fine, handmade cigar sells for $5 or more.

7. The wrapper is responsible for the taste and aroma of a cigar.

8. Every cigar except the custom shapes, use a mold to make them uniform. There are a few dozen standard shapes.

HOW A CIGAR IS MADE

in diameter, round, and the color of the wrapper are used to as a cap on the cigar. The circle of tobacco is laid out on the table and the cigar is placed onto the center of the circle the way you'd put a pen into an inkwell. A vegetable glue is used to seal the end cap. This cap holds the wrapper on so it doesn't unwind! Keep this

Right: **Putting the wrapper onto a Montecristo No.2 requires great skill. The cigars held together with the binder leaf are still in the mold.**

Bottom: **Robusto size being sorted by color so all the cigars in a given box will look and taste the same.**

HOW A CIGAR IS MADE

Left: The dried leaves are moistened under a spray before they are rolled into cigars. It is impossible to make cigars with dry tobacco leaves.

Below: After moistening, the bundles of wrapper are hung in special racks to uniformly soak in the moisture before they are flattened out prior to being used.

Right: After being removed from the drying rack, the bundles are taken apart and once again sorted by color.

Bottom, facing page: The moistened, flattened capa (wrapper) leaves are bunched by shade and weight and are sent to the rollers.

HOW A CIGAR IS MADE

HOW A CIGAR IS MADE

in mind when cutting off the end of the cigar before smoking it. You don't want to cut off this cap. Usually as you smoke the cigar and the end becomes wet, the remainder of this cap ends up in your mouth or sticking out. It is easily removed with your fingers and disposed of in the ashtray. If you have cut off the cap, the cigar will unravel (very slightly) and when you try to remove what you think is the cap, you start unwinding the wrapper.

The cigar is now ready for color grading and is usually bunched in batches of 25 or 50, tied together with a wide cloth reusable band about 1-2" in width, and stored in cedar cabinets until the sorters need them. In cheaper handmade cigars, this final sorting is eliminated.

After the final sorting by color, the cigars are tested for length and ring gauge. Then bands are attached and the cigars are boxed.

A single primitive tool is used to confirm the length and (below) the ring gauge of the cigars before they are boxed. Obviously, if they are too long or too thick they will not fit 25 to the box.

HOW A CIGAR IS MADE

Usually the identification of the cigar is not known by the roller. In Cuba where there always seems to be a shortage of something, the cigars are ringed only after the rest of the packaging is assembled. I have often seen Partagas rings being removed from cigars with Romeo y Julieta being substituted. When I asked the foreman why, I was told that they had Romeo y Julieta boxes but no Partagas boxes! This was a common practice in the old days (before 1960) when cigars were ringed according to orders received from overseas. To this day cigars are made, stored and sorted by size and shape in Cuba.

A bundle of wrapper leaves usually contains 25-40 separate leaves. This produces 50-80 wrappers.

The perfect wrapper is half a leaf which has only major veins running in one direction. These veins are invisible on the other side of the leaf and make a wonderful cigar.

HOW A CIGAR IS MADE

NOT ALL CIGARS ARE SHAPED BY A MOLD. I have a cigar made for me that is bat-shaped. No mold for this shape exists. The lady who makes them rolls them in strips of newspaper until they *harden*. She happens to be an exceptional roller and worked as a public demonstrator in the cigar store in the Marina Hemingway Complex in Havana. She will make any shape and any formula providing she has the tobacco. I had to supply my own *capa* because she had no capa long enough for the 9" cigar I wanted (nor was her stock dark enough for she could have used two leaves as wrapper for a long cigar). My mouth waters as I write this and I am looking forward to lighting one up tonight after dinner!

At the present time rollers and capa are at a premium. Skilled rollers, like the lady from Marina Hemingway, are very rare. Perhaps one in 500 rollers are good enough to roll cigars free-hand and have them look uniform and draw easily. Obviously the bat shape and the pyramid shapes have to have the tobacco distributed unevenly throughout the cigar...and this takes a lot of talent.

The final inspection of Montecristo No.2's at the Partagas factory includes a visual inspection of each cigar as it is placed into the box. Only the most experienced rollers are used for this final inspection.

HOW A CIGAR IS MADE

Above: If you take a fine, long filler cigar apart you will only find full leaves of varying sizes and colors.

There is no way you can learn how to roll a cigar from a book. It's a hands-on profession..and always has been. Rollers have always been pampered. In many cigar factories readers keep the rollers entertained by reading books out loud as the rollers do their thing. This tradition has gradually disappeared and has been replaced with recorded music.

The manufacture of cigars by machine is simple. Tobacco cut into pieces about

The dried unfertilized seed pod below which is the fertilized and dry seed pod. The seeds are the specks coming from a ruptured seed pod. Each seed produced a tobacco plant.

HOW A CIGAR IS MADE

HOW A CIGAR IS MADE

1. It takes five years of age for fine tobacco to be made into an exceptional cigar. This custom is disappearing as the cigar market boom has produced inexperienced smokers.
2. Tobacco is usually grown far from the factories that roll it.
3. Rollers make from 75-150 cigars per day by hand.
4. Don't cut the cap from the end of the cigar or the wrapper might unravel.
5. All cigars are made by size; the market and supply of rings, bands and boxes determine the ultimate designation of the brand. Thus the ratings found in cigar magazines are useless.
6. Most cigars are molded, but molds are not necessary for skilled craftsmen.
7. There are machines which can produce 1,000 good cigars a day. Mass produced cigars have their devotees, don't look down your nose at them. They probably know more about which cigars taste best for them than you do.

The author has the nasty habit of cutting cigars open to verify their contents. This cigar, sold as a fine Dominican cigar, was merely machine made with cut tobacco as filler

HOW A CIGAR IS MADE

After rolling, the cigars are bundled in 50's and aged for various lengths of time. At present, Cuban cigars are not aged for more than a few months because of Cuba's dire need for cash.

1" square is placed onto a belt with binder. A quick roll movement of about 12" in each direction produces a cigar held together by a binder. The wrapper can also be applied by machine or finished by hand. The scraps of tobacco may also be leaves. There are many variations of the above.

The use of HTL (homogenized tobacco leaf) for binders and wrappers plus machine made cigar capabilities has enabled the mass market cigar to maintain its very low price when compared to a completely hand-made cigar. I have many friends who prefer the cheapest of cigars, even smoking Italian cigars which are single rolled leaves allowed to dry to the utmost hardness. They only use very oily tobacco and they are very strong. People who like these cigars usually don't smoke anything else.

DON'T LOOK AT THESE SMOKERS WITH DISDAIN...RATHER LOOK AT THEM AS TRUE CIGAR CONNOISSEURS. They know what they want in a cigar. Most of the new cigar smokers know neither what they want nor what they are smoking. In tests I have made dozens of times, most cigar smokers cannot tell the difference between a machine made Mexican cigar and a totally hand-made Cuban.

HOW A CIGAR IS MADE

This machine makes cigars. Cut tobacco is placed on the end of the top. In front (see below) a binder leaf is laid out. A quick back-and-forth movement of the handle produces a cigar without a wrapper. A wrapper leaf can then be used to finish the cigar or it can be put on by hand.

This cutter puts a V-shaped slit in the top of the cigar. The photo below shows a side view of this antique cutter.

HOW TO ENJOY SMOKING A CIGAR

There are as many ways to smoke a cigar as your imagination can conceive. So let's take it step-by-step.

CUTTING OFF THE END

Mass produced cigars may already have the end punctured. This enables you to light it up immediately without cutting off the end.

For fine cigars the maxim is to *cut off as little as possible in order to get an easy draw.* If you cut off too much, thus removing the cap, the cigar might unravel, but usually the cigar is put into your mouth before it has a chance to unravel, and, once it is wet, the wrapper does not unravel.

There are five basic types of cigar cutters: the *guillotine* cutters are the most common and they vary from cheap, plastic-framed give-aways which tobacconists give free to

This rounded scissors can do it all. It enables you to cut large cigars in half, if necessary. No other cutter can do this.

This guillotine cutter is the most practical for carrying in your pocket. It is shown open above and closed below. This cutter has served the author for 31 years.

HOW TO ENJOY SMOKING A CIGAR

their good customers, to desk-top models shaped in various ways; the *scissors* cigar cutters are the best for most cigars and they vary from common scissors to scissors with rounded blades; the *hole punch* is a very fine method of preparing a cigar for smoking. The punch can be made of

An old guillotine cutter which is limited by the 48 gauge of its opening diameter.

This modern drill is stainless steel and razor sharp. It is twirled on the end of the cigar and when withdrawn, it takes a round chunk of the cigar out. It comes with a matching cover so it can be safely carried in your pocket. It works very well with thick cigars.

solid gold or stainless steel but the drill is always a razor sharp stainless steel which is rotated on top of the cigar to remove about 1/4" of tobacco as deep as you want it to be. The *ultimate* cigar cutter is the one used by the rollers. It is a bed upon which the cigar is laid. A stop determines the length of the cigar and the non-smoking end of the cigar is cut off with a sharp blade which rotates as it is hand activated. The blades are removable and can be sharpened. By laying your cigar down in the opposite

HOW TO ENJOY SMOKING A CIGAR

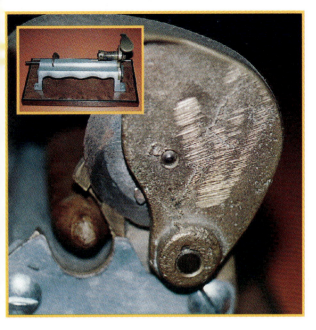

The ultimate cutter is that which is used by the rollers themselves. The rotating razor-sharp circular blade neatly slices off the end of the cigar. The insert shows the cutter without a cigar.

direction, the tip can be cut off exactly the same length every time you cut one. I have several of these cutters, all having been gifts from cigar factories. The ones I have are more than 100 years old and have traditionally been given to favorite visitors. The final type of cutter is a *notch* cutter. This takes a V-shaped gash out of the cigar and is favored by everyone who uses one PROVIDING the top of the cigar they are smoking is flat.

Since I smoke torpedoes, pyramids, and other non-flat ended cigars, I use the round scissors or the *ultimate* cigar cutter used by the rollers.

The lesson to be learned is to cut the end of the cigar immediately before you light it. Don't cut the end far in advance as the wrapper might begin to unravel. I know of no fine cigar which can be smoked without cutting off the end.

HOW TO ENJOY SMOKING A CIGAR

WHAT DO YOU DO WITH THE RING?

The question of removing the ring or not is moot. Do what you want to do; it has nothing to do with the taste or aroma of smoking. Personally, I always remove the ring before I smoke the cigar. Sometimes I regret doing this because infrequently the ring has been inadvertently glued to the wrapper and the wrapper is torn as the ring is removed. I happen to have a personal distaste for leaving on the ring because it might burn if you smoke the cigar as short as I smoke mine.

Historically, romantics wrote that fine men and women wore white gloves and the rings were used to protect their gloves from being stained by the tobacco. This is probably untrue because the cigar rings have rarely been large enough to protect a finger from making contact with the tobacco.

Cheap cigars are not ringed because the ring and labor to put it on are relatively too expensive. Fine cigars are usually ringed as an advertising gimmick as well as to identify the cigar should the smoker buy several brands of cigar of the same shape. Probably the basic reason for putting rings on cigars was to keep up with the mode.

Early in the life of cigars, they were sold without identification as to country of origin or manufacturer. In order to make the cigar look more luxurious, Cuban entrepreneurs put rings on their cigars. The first big names in cigars rarely made all their own cigars. Instead they bought cigars from others and merely identified them by putting on their own rings. This separated their cigars from the cigars of the men who made them, thus enabling them to get more money per cigar than their supplier. Why does Tiffany autograph every piece of jewelry? Perhaps they learned the value of advertising their name from the Cuban cigar manufacturers. In any case Enzo Infante's book takes you through the history of cigar rings and box labels.

To remove the ring simply catch the end of the ring with your nail and gently unwind it. If it gets stuck because the glue overflowed onto the wrapper, you lost! A good trick is to try pulling the ring off the cigar without opening the ring. It works very well with old cigars (more than 4 years old), but not always.

HOW TO ENJOY SMOKING A CIGAR

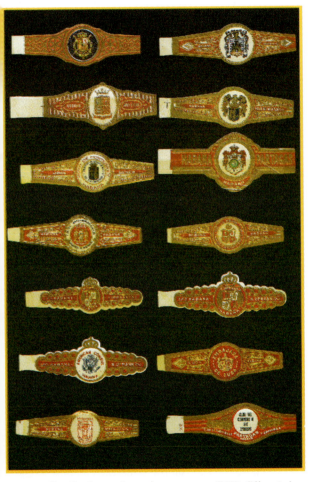

There are literally thousands, maybe as many as 50,000, different cigar bands which adorned Cuban cigars. They serve no function except identification and adornment.

HOW TO ENJOY SMOKING A CIGAR

LIGHTING THE CIGAR

You have selected your cigar and you are psychologically prepared to rest, relax, think or kill your appetite so you'll lose weight. For whatever reason, be sure you are READY to enjoy a fine cigar.

Before cutting the end, stick the open end into your nostril and take a few slow, deep breaths. The smell should be familiar because you have done this before and learned what a good cigar smells like. If it doesn't smell good, put it aside and give it to one of your amateur cigar-smoking friends who won't know the difference. After finding the proper cigar by smell and feel, look at the wrapper by reflected light and admire the slight sheen, soft-to-the-squeeze feel and lovely color. You should have learned what to expect in taste by the shade of the wrapper. Now put the cigar in your mouth after cutting the end. Take four or five slow, deep draws before you light it. Savor the taste. It, too, should be characteristic of a fine cigar. If it is bitter, the cigar hasn't aged enough! Now is the time to light it.

Ideally you have had boxes of fine cigars before and you saved the wooden sheet which separates the two rows of cigars. Using a scissors, cut the sheet into strips which you will light from a fire source and then light your cigar from this burning cedar strip. For some reason or other, cedar and cigars were made for each other. Cedar boxes, cedar cigar wrappings and cedar matches are all flavor enhancers for cigars!

There are two ways of lighting a cigar. In Cuba I have often been entertained by the Habanos (government cigar monopoly) at a fine restaurant. After the dinner, I usually am presented with an array of Cohibas from which to select one for my after-dinner smoke. The cigar waiter (like a trained wine waiter), clips off the end with curved scissors and holds a long piece of burning cedar to the end of the cigar, slowly rotating it. In between holding the cigar in the yellow section of the flame, he rotates the cigar in a wrist-rolling gesture. This whole procedure takes less than 2 minutes after which he hands me a perfectly lit cigar. I have witnessed this a hundred times and I have NEVER been able to duplicate it!

I use a butane lighter or a piece of cedar. My wife doesn't like me to use the cedar... *"I'm afraid the end might*

HOW TO ENJOY SMOKING A CIGAR

drop off and set the rug on fire"... I light the cigar slowly; I rotate it as I draw and examine the end after a few draws to be sure the cigar is uniformly lit. If you don't start uniformly, the cigar will burn unevenly. The first smoke emanating from a freshly lit cigar is heavenly. My wife comes over to breathe in the first fumes. This is the true test of a Havana. You'll be able to tell a Havana cigar just by the aroma once you learn the difference.

Smoke the cigar, take a drag every 30 seconds or so, but try to keep it lit. By smoking too slowly, the cigar goes out. This is not a serious problem at all, it's just bothersome. I rarely have a cigar go out, but then again, I smoke too fast.

A fine cigar made with long filler should establish an ash at least 1/2" before it become dangerous to fall off onto your shirt, lap, table or tie. Remove the ash by GENTLY rubbing the ash off into the ash tray. The longer the ash the better the smoke. The ash keeps the cigar burning slowly and uniformly. I had a friend with a sense of humor. He inserted a stiff, fine 4" long wire (like paper-clip wire) into the end of the cigar. He would light the cigar and wouldn't flick off the ash because the wire would keep the ash from falling off. This was always an attention getting act!

A mark of a prime quality cigar is a uniform ring of burning with a very tiny ring of black at the base of the ash.

I infrequently leave a portion of a cigar over for the next day. But when I do, I have no problem after the first few puffs. Most writers advise you to throw the cigar away. I don't.

When you have finished smoking, it is polite to properly dispose of the ashes and the butt of the cigar. If you are done smoking a cigar simply allow it to go out by itself. Don't squash it the way cigarette smokers do. A cigar will produce a lovely aroma even as it dies. But a squashed cigar gives off a foul odor as if to protest the indignity of its death! Allowing the butt to remain in an ashtray overnight is an invitation to a stale tobacco smell that is far from inviting. Immediately after smoking a cigar, I take the ash tray into the bathroom and half fill the ash tray with tap water. I then flush the toilet and once the water in the toilet bowl starts moving I dump in the contents of the ash tray. I usually can rinse the ash tray with another watering before the toilet is finished flushing. This prevents the ashes from adhering to the sides of the toilet bowl. If you simply throw the ashes

HOW TO ENJOY SMOKING A CIGAR

into a toilet bowl and then flush it, a ring will persist and it is difficult to remove without a brush.

When I finish smoking in my living room, I always open a few doors or windows to flush the smoke out of the room. The same is true in a hotel room. I don't enjoy sleeping in a smoke-laden room. But I have friends that do!

If you live in a two-story home, smoke rises, so if you smoke downstairs, expect to smell it upstairs!

BE POLITE. THE SMELL OF CIGARS IS NOT PLEASING TO EVERYONE. YOU HAVE NO RIGHT TO POLLUTE SOMEONE ELSE'S AIR SPACE. I never smoke in a restaurant or public place (except a hotel lobby in an obscure corner). I abhor cigarette smoke when I am eating (I even hate it when I'm not eating!); I don't mind pipe smoke, but I know many people who object to cigar and pipe smoking. They should be respected. You can't enjoy a cigar knowing it is making somebody else uncomfortable. A cigar should be your ticket to an hour of peace, comfort and, perhaps, solitude. I enjoy smoking alone, but I have often been in business meetings where cigars were lit up. I learned from a very famous businessman that cigar smoking at business meetings is tactical. If you are questioned about something that requires some thought, merely put your cigar in your mouth, but don't puff. Then fumble for a light, light the cigar, take a deep draw, remove the cigar from your mouth and look at it admiringly. Then shift your gaze to your adversary, look him in the eye and answer his question. If you can't or won't answer his query, just say *"Why are you trying to ruin my enjoyment of this fine cigar?"* I've tried this several times and it always works! Your adversary will never ask the same question again, nor will he be aggressive.

THE CIGAR BOX

Most fine cigars come in wooden boxes with fancy labels. Some come in cedar boxes, a few in glass containers, some individually boxed, in aluminum or glass tubes, or in individual cardboard boxes. There are some cardboard boxes which have 3 or 5 cigars in them.

Cigar boxes do little for the cigar. Heavy cedar boxes probably impart a taste to the cigar if the cigar is already good. It doesn't help a bad cigar. Cigar containers do not protect cigars from drying out. They are merely protectors

HOW TO ENJOY SMOKING A CIGAR

of the cigars from physical harm and are merchandising gimmicks. The hobby of collecting cigar boxes, cigar labels and cigar rings is well established. I even collect the old lithographic stones from which these fancy labels were made in the old times.

You cannot judge the quality of the cigar by the quality of the container. The best cigars come in solid wooden boxes with no paper covers or labels. This quality look is actually a production tool. We already know that cigars are made by size and are labelled according to orders or convenience. Since the totally wooden boxes are branded with a red hot iron, a single inventory of sizes can serve many brands and can be completed quickly. It takes 17 days to make a Montecristo box with all it labels. It takes 3 hours to make a wooden box including the hot stamping.

Of course, empty cigar boxes have been used for years to hold bills, nails, paper clips, and just about anything else that will fit into them.

HOW TO HOLD A CIGAR

The way a cigar should be held depends upon the size of the cigar initially, and the size of the stub. Most men hold a lit cigar between the thumb and the first two fingers. When the stub is too short, they use their thumb and their index finger. A cigar should never be held between the first two fingers. That is too feminine and cigars are not feminine.

There are, however, very small cigars which are just glorified cigarettes. These can be held any way as they are not real cigars.

Women who smoke cigars are entitled to hold them any way that suits them. Women who smoke cigars are a special breed. Danish women have been smoking cigars for generations. They hold cigars between their two fingers but they never smoke large cigars (nor do they smoke tiny cigars).

The bottom line, of course, is to hold the cigar in a manner most comfortable for your hand and the cigar length. Sometimes I have a very long and heavy cigar which I must hold between my thumb and first three fingers. Just make yourself comfortable and safe. You don't want to drop a lit cigar as it is dangerous. Be careful. Hopefully this book contains all you need to know to enjoy a fine cigar at it's fullest. Enjoy!

HOW TO ENJOY SMOKING A CIGAR

HOW TO ENJOY A CIGAR

1. Cut off the end of the cigar properly with a special tool. There are five basic kinds of cigar cutters. Find one that suits your needs.
2. Smell the cigar by putting the cut end into your nostril.
3. Taste the cigar before lighting it by drawing on it a few times. The proper taste and smell before lighting can identify a good or bad cigar once you get some experience.
4. Removing the ring is up to you. If you remove it be careful not to tear the wrapper.
5. Light the cigar with a burning piece of cedar or with a butane lighter. Light the end of the cigar uniformly.
6. A cigar can be lit after it has gone out. Cigars can usually be saved to be finished another day.
7. Discard cigar butts and ashes in a toilet. Don't throw them into a garbage receptacle as they might start a fire and they will smell badly.
8. Don't smoke in situations where you might make others uncomfortable.
9. Cigars can be useful during business meetings, both as gifts and as time consumers allowing you time to think.
10. Do not inhale a cigar; you get enough smoke into your lungs from the second hand smoke.
11. Hold a cigar in any manner that is safe and comfortable. Usually a man uses his thumb and first two fingers.
12. Never warm a cigar by running a flame over its wrapper. This was supposedly done long ago to kill insects and evaporate the sticky gum. My grandfather said it made the sticky gum non-adhesive and more comfortable to smoke. I never found a cigar with insects, adhesives or any reason which could be satisfied with an open flame.